Macmillan McGraw-Hill

Math Connects

4

Problem-Solving
Practice Workbook

Macmillan/McGraw-Hill

TO THE STUDENT This *Problem-Solving Practice Workbook* gives you additional examples and problems for the concept exercises in each lesson. The exercises are designed to help you study mathematics by reinforcing important skills needed to succeed in the everyday world. The materials are organized by chapter and lesson, with one Problem-Solving Practice worksheet for every lesson in *Math Connects, Grade 4*.

Always keep your workbook handy. Along with you textbook, daily homework, and class notes, the completed *Problem-Solving Practice Workbook* can help you in reviewing for quizzes and tests.

TO THE TEACHER These worksheets are the same ones found in the Chapter Resource Masters for *Math Connects, Grade 4*. The answers to these worksheets are available at the end of each Chapter Resource Masters booklet.

The McGraw-Hill Companies

 Macmillan/McGraw-Hill

Send all inquiries to:
Macmillan/McGraw-Hill
8787 Orion Place
Columbus, OH 43240

ISBN: 978-0-02-107292-7
MHID: 0-02-107292-2   *Problem-Solving Practice Workbook, Grade 4*

Printed in the United States of America.

3 4 5 6 7 8 9 10 RHR 14 13 12 11 10

CONTENTS

1-1

Problem-Solving Practice

Place Value Through Hundred Thousands

Solve.

1. Michael says he has used 42,567 pencils since he started school. Maria wants to be sure she heard the number correctly. Write 42,567 in word form and in expanded form for Maria.

_____

_____

2. Emily and Inez found a treasure map that shows the location of gold coins. They want to show their friends how much gold they can find. Write the number in standard form. 200,000 + 70,000 + 4,000 + 600 + 90 + 3 _____

3. Javier and Nick want to start a dog-walking business after school. They made 1,236 flyers to hand out around their neighborhood. Write the number in word form and in expanded form.

_____

_____

4. Union Township has a population of 1<u>7</u>2,650. What is the value of the underlined digit? _____

5. School District 270 has 84,572 students. Last year there were 1,000 fewer students. In five years, the District expects to have 2,000 more students than they have now. How many students did School District 270 have last year? _____ How many students do they expect to have in five years?_____

6. Jan's grandfather was a pilot. He estimates that he has flown 460,500 miles in his life. When Jan told her mother about this, Jan said 406,500 miles. Jan's mother said she should get her numbers right. What mistake did Jan make? How can Jan fix it?

_____

_____

_____

Name _____ Date _____

Problem-Solving Practice

Place Value Through Millions

Solve.

1. Hannah read that 11,765,825 people saw the L.A. Lakers play last season. Chris wants to be sure he heard the number correctly. Write 11,765,825 in word form and in expanded form for Chris.

   _____

   _____

   _____

2. There are approximately 200,000,000 + 90,000,000 + 8,000,000 + 800,000 + 60,000 + 9,000 + 500 + 2 people living in the United States. Write the number in standard form. _____

3. Approximately 37,124,871 people live in California. Write the number in word form and in expanded form.

   _____

   _____

   _____

   _____

4. The pirate movie made $1<u>3</u>5,634,554 in one weekend. What is the value of the underlined digit? _____

5. In 1982, about 40,020,000 people watched the Super Bowl on television. In 2006 there were 50,000,000 more viewers. In 2011, television experts believe 5,000,000 fewer people than in 2006 will watch the game. How many people watched the Super Bowl in 2006? _____ How many people do experts believe will watch in 2011? _____

6. American car makers produce 5,650,000 cars each year. In a report, Ben wrote that Americans made 6,550,000 cars. What mistake did Ben make? How can he fix it?

   _____

   _____

   _____

   _____

Name _____ Date _____

Problem-Solving Practice

Compare Whole Numbers

Solve.

1. Charles is moving from Springfield, which has 482,653 people, to Greenville, which has 362,987. Is he moving to a larger or smaller city? Explain.

   _____

   _____

2. The Denver Mint made 2,638,800,000 pennies. The Philadelphia Mint made 2,806,000,000 pennies. Which mint made more pennies?

   _____

3. About 450,000 people lived in Maryville in 2000. In 2005, about 467,000 people lived in Maryville. Did the number of people living in Maryville get larger or smaller?

   _____

4. In 1950, bike stores sold about 205,850 bikes. In 2000, bike stores sold about 185,000 bikes. Is the number of bikes being sold getting larger or smaller?

   _____

5. In 2000, about 290,000,000 cans of soda were sold each day. In 1970, about 65,000,000 cans were sold each day. Were more cans of soda sold in 2000 or 1970? Explain.

   _____

   _____

6. Allison found out that the average American works about 2,100 hours a year. The average French worker works about 1,650 hours a year. Who works more hours?

   _____

1–5

Problem-Solving Practice

Order Whole Numbers

Solve.

1. For the state high school basketball tournament, the teams are divided into groups based on the size of their high school. Order these high schools from most students to least. Then name the two the largest high schools.

   Fremont: 2,759   Kingsville: 1,865
   Jefferson: 2,341   La Plata: 2,056

   _____

   _____

   _____

2. Madison wants to know which sports are most popular in California. She reads a list that shows how many kids play each sport. Order the sports from most players to least to help show Madison which sports are popular.

   Soccer: 3,875,026   Lacrosse: 900,765
   Surfing: 250,982   Basketball: 2,025,351

3. Tyler wondered how many people voted in the United States Presidential elections. He wants to know which year had the fewest voters in these four elections. Order the election years from least to greatest number of voters.

   2004: 122,295,345   1996: 96,456,345
   2000: 105,586,274   1992: 104,405,155

4. Rosa's science teacher challenged the class to reduce the amount of electricity they used. First, students needed to find out how much they were using. Order the students from who used the most electricity to who used the least.

   Rosa: 3,056 kwh   Anna: 3,098 kwh
   Austin: 3,125 kwh   Robert: 3,105 kwh

1-6

Problem-Solving Practice

Round Whole Numbers

Solve.

1. Taipei 101 in Taiwan is the world's tallest building at 1,673 feet tall. How tall is this building when rounded to the nearest hundred? The nearest thousand?

   _____

2. The Golden Gate Bridge spans about 4,224 feet. Brian says the bridge spans about 4,000 feet. Samantha says it spans about 4,200 feet. Their teacher says they are both correct. How is this possible? _____

   _____

3. The Lake Mead reservoir at the Hoover Dam covers 157,900 acres. How large is Lake Mead rounded to the nearest hundred thousand?

   _____

4. Ricardo estimates there are 10,000 balls in the ball pit at the park. His father helps him count the 12,345 balls. Is Ricardo's estimate good if he rounds to the ten thousand? Is it good if he rounds to the thousand? Explain. _____

   _____

   _____

   _____

5. Experts estimate that there are 500,000 leopards living in the wild. If we were able to count all the leopards and found 527,863 leopards, would the 500,000 estimate be a good estimate? Explain.

   _____

   _____

6. Gabriella has 15,467 coins she has collected from around the world. Her friends asked her about how many coins were in her collection. What would be a good answer for her to tell them? Explain.

   _____

   _____

Problem-Solving Practice

Algebra: Addition Properties and Subtraction Rules

Solve.

1. While bird watching, Gabrielle saw 6 robins, 4 cardinals, and 3 blue jays. Chase saw 3 robins, 6 blue jays and 4 cardinals. Who saw more birds? _____

   _____

2. For homework, Brooke has 15 math problems, 5 social studies problems, and 9 science problems. Use mental math to determine how many problems she has for homework. Tell what property you used. _____

   _____

   _____

   _____

3. Jose needs to leave in 85 minutes to go to a movie. Before he leaves, he has to finish his homework, which takes 22 minutes; clean his room, which takes 18 minutes; walk the dog, which takes 35 minutes; and take out the trash, which takes 5 minutes. Does Jose have enough time to do all of these before he leaves? Find the sum mentally. Tell what property you used.

   _____

   _____

   _____

   _____

   _____

4. A soccer team scored 2 goals in the first half. If they won the game by a score of 2 to 1, how many goals did they score in the second half? Tell what property you used.

   _____

   _____

Name _____ Date _____

Problem-Solving Practice

Estimate Sums and Differences

Solve.

1. The parking lot in front of the school has 53 parking spaces. The parking lot in the back of the school has 38 spaces. About how many parking spaces are there? Round your answer to the nearest ten.

   _____

2. A total of 691 people attended the school play. 521 people attended the band concert. About how many more people attended the play than the concert? Round your answer to the nearest hundred.

   _____

3. A large pizza costs $8. A medium drink costs $2. About how much does a large pizza and 2 medium drinks cost?

   _____

4. On Wednesday, 37 students played kickball. On Thursday, 28 students played kickball. About how many students played kickball on Wednesday and Thursday? Round your answer to the nearest ten.

   _____

5. The highest point in Texas, Guadalupe Peak, is 8,749 feet high. The highest Point in California, Mount McKinley, is 14,494 feet high. About how much higher is Mount McKinley then Guadalupe Peak? Round your answer to the nearest thousand.

   _____

6. Christina spent $6 on a ticket to the fair. She also spent $5 on food and $3 for the rides. About how much did Christina spend at the fair?

   _____

2–4

Problem-Solving Practice

Add Whole Numbers

Solve.

1. In 2003 the population of Cedar Park, Texas, was 41,482 and the population of College Station, Texas, was 73,536. What was the combined population of Cedar Park and College Station?

   _____

2. A school fundraiser made $877 on pizza sales and $487 on wrapping paper sales. How much money did the fundraiser make?

   _____

3. A zoo has two elephants, Sally and Joe. Sally weighs 7,645 pounds and Joe weighs 12,479 pounds. How much do Sally and Joe weigh in all?

   _____

4. In December, New York City had 3 inches of snow. In January and February the city had 8 inches of snow. In March, the city had 2 inches of snow. How many inches of snow fell during December, January, February, and March?

   _____

5. At a library 1,324 children's books, 1,510 fiction books, and 912 non-fiction books were checked out. How many books were checked out of the library?

   _____

6. Colin spent 35 minutes mowing the lawn, 22 minutes trimming the bushes, and 12 minutes watering the flowers. How long did it take Colin to do the yard work?

   _____

2-5

Problem-Solving Practice

Subtract Whole Numbers

Solve.

1. There are 635 people in the stadium when the football game starts. Before the game is over, 213 people leave early. How many people remained to see the end of the game?

   _____

2. Miranda buys lunch for herself and a friend for $14. If she hands the cashier $20, how much change will she get back?

   _____

3. In 2006, it had been 230 years since the United States became a nation. In what year did the United States become a nation?

   _____

4. Sierra took 83 free throws during the basketball season. If she missed 34 of them, how many free throws did she make?

   _____

5. Alicia had $112 in her bank account. She bought a present for her sister for $22 and a present for her brother for $24. How much money does she have in her account now?

   _____

6. As a promotion, a minor league baseball team is giving out 1,250 free hats. If 2,359 people attended the game, how many did not get a hat?

   _____

Name _____ Date _____

Problem-Solving Practice

Subtract Across Zeros

Solve.

1. In a 90-minute soccer game Jorge played 72 minutes. How long was he on the sideline?

   _____

2. If 700 tickets were sold to a concert and only 587 people attended, how many people bought a ticket but did not go?

   _____

3. In a chess tournament, 400 players take part in the first round. During the second round, 274 players take part. How many players did not make the second round?

   _____

4. The Amazon River is 4,000 miles long. The Snake River is 1,038 miles long. How much longer is the Amazon River than the Snake River?

   _____

5. Logan has a gift card for $200. He spends $45 on Monday and $61 on Tuesday. How much money is left on his gift card?

   _____

6. Luisa takes $75 to the amusement park. She spends $29 on a ticket, $13 on food, and $22 on a T-shirt. How much money does she have left?

   _____

3-1

Problem-Solving Practice

Collect and Organize Data

Solve.

1. Make a tally chart for the number of students in the third-, fourth-, and fifth-grade classes: 26, 25, 27, 27, 26, 28, 27.

   _____

2. Use the data in your tally chart from Exercise 1. Which class size is most common?

   _____

3. Make a tally chart and a frequency table for the number of books read by students during the summer: 4, 5, 7, 2, 4, 5, 6, 7, 8, 4, 5, 3. How many students took part in this survey?

   _____

4. If another student is added to the survey and says she read 7 books, how would you change your tally chart and frequency table to show this?

   _____

5. Make a tally chart and a frequency table for the data showing amount of time it takes students to do their homework: 35 min, 1 hour, $1\frac{1}{2}$ hours, 45 min, 60 min, 30 min, 45 min, 90 min, $\frac{1}{2}$ hour. According to your frequency table, what is the longest time it takes the students to do their homework?

   _____

   _____

6. What is the difference between the greatest amount of time and the least amount of time spent doing homework?

   _____

3-2

Problem-Solving Practice

Find Mode, Median, and Outliers

Normal Temperatures in January (°F)				
Texas 43	Nebraska 21	Minnesota 12	Michigan 23	Illinois 21
Oklahoma 36	S. Dakota 22	Iowa 19	Indiana 26	Missouri 26
Kansas 25	N. Dakota 9	Wisconsin 20	Ohio 26	Arkansas 39

Use data from the table to solve.

1. Find the **median** and the **mode** of the data.

_____

_____

2. Find the **outlier** of the data.

_____

3. Which three states have the same normal temperature in January?

_____

4. Are there any outliers in this data? Explain.

_____

_____

5. Find the median and range for the three states with the **lowest** temperature.

_____

6. Find the median and range for the three states with the **highest** temperature.

_____

Name _____ Date _____

Problem-Solving Practice

Line Plots

Solve. Use a line plot to help you organize your information.

Jennifer wants to know how hard her friends thought the extra credit math problem was. She asked them how many tries it took them to solve the problem. She made a chart of her information.

Friends	Answer
Dylan	3
Allison	5
Jose	12
Olivia	4
Jesse	6
Chelsea	4
Logan	6
Maria	7
Trevor	4

1. How many tries was the most common answer? _____

2. What was the median number of tries? _____

3. One friend's answer was very different from the other friends. How many tries did the one very different friend take? _____

Hunter wants to know how old his classmates were when they learned how to swim. He took a survey and made a chart of his data:

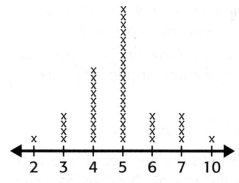

4. What age was the most common age to learn to swim? _____

5. What ages had the same number of students learn to swim?

_____

6. What age was very different from all the other students' ages?

_____

Name _____ Date _____

Problem-Solving Practice

Bar Graphs

Determine the best graph to show the data.

1. You ask your friends about their favorite kinds of books. If you made a bar graph of the data, how would you label each axis?

   _____

   _____

   _____

2. Your family takes a road trip for vacation. You write down the number of times you see different state license plates. You saw Texas plates 42 times, New Mexico plates 36 times, Arizona plates 32 times, and California plates 19 times. If you make a bar graph of the data, how many bars would your graph have? How long would the bar for California be compared to Texas?

   _____

3. You want to make a graph of your test scores in different school subjects. How many bars would your graph shows? How would they be labeled?

   _____

   _____

4. Julio wants to make a bar graph that shows his friends' favorite types of music. He polls 12 friends. Half say their favorite is pop music. One-third say they like rock music the best. The rest say they like country. How long will the bar for pop music be compared to the bar for country?

   _____

5. Kim wants to make a graph that shows the number of runs each player on her softball team made this season. Describe how she could label each axis.

   _____

   _____

   _____

Name _____ Date _____

Problem-Solving Practice

Bar and Double Bar Graphs

For Exercises 1–2, use the bar graph that shows class election results.

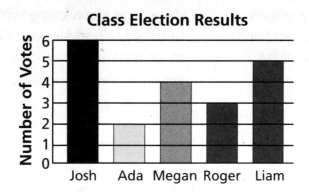

Class Election Results

1. How many more votes did Josh get than Roger? Explain how you know. _____

2. How many votes did Ada and Roger get? Explain how you know.

_____

Use a separate sheet of paper to make a bar graph. Then solve.

3. Maurice made a bar graph to show the number of people wearing sneakers, boots, and regular shoes in his classroom. Fifteen students are wearing sneakers. Eight are wearing regular shoes, and six students are wearing boots. Make a bar graph to show the data. How many students are in Maurice's class?

_____

4. Betina looked at Maurice's bar graph. She guessed that the number of students who are wearing regular shoes and boots is greater than the number of students wearing sneakers. Is Betina's

guess correct? _____

Explain. _____

Name _____ Date _____

Problem-Solving Practice

Determine Possible Outcomes

Solve.

1. You spin a spinner with 4 equal sections marked 1–4. Then you spin another spinner with 3 equal sections colored red, blue, and yellow. What are all of the possible outcomes?

   _____

   _____

   _____

2. The Boardwalk Shop sells souvenir shirts. The shirts come with long sleeves or short sleeves. The shirts come in white, gray, and blue. What are all of the different kinds of shirts?

   _____

   _____

3. Karen throws a dart at a target with 5 equal sections marked 1–5. She then throws a dart at a target with two equal sections colored green and blue. What are all of the possible outcomes?

   _____

   _____

   _____

4. Boardwalk Burgers sells burgers made from beef, turkey, chicken, or soy. Burgers can have no cheese, Swiss cheese, or American cheese. How many different choices are there?

   _____

   _____

   _____

Solve. Use any strategy.

5. The Target Toss Game has 6 rings. The first ring is worth 4 points, the second ring is worth 8 points, and the third ring is worth 12 points. If the pattern continues, what is the sixth ring worth?

   _____

   Strategy: _____

6. In a recent year, $\frac{11}{100}$ of all U.S. vacations included time at the beach, $\frac{6}{100}$ included time at sports events, and $\frac{8}{100}$ included time at theme parks. Write these activities in order from least to most popular?

   _____

   _____

   Strategy: _____

Name _____ Date _____

Problem-Solving Practice

Probability

Describe the probability of each outcome. Use *certain*, *likely*, *equally likely*, *unlikely*, or *impossible*.

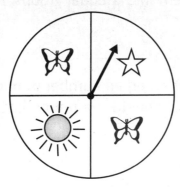

1. spinning a star or a sun

_____

2. spinning a butterfly

_____

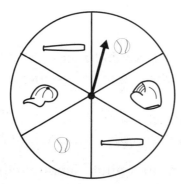

3. spinning a baseball or bat

_____

4. spinning a catcher's mitt

_____

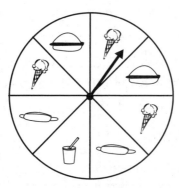

5. spinning a hot dog or a hamburger

_____

6. probability of spinning a soda

_____

4–1

Problem-Solving Practice

Relate Multiplication and Division

Solve.

1. Min has 10 photos. She separates them into 2 equal groups. How many photos are in each group?

   _____

2. Kara has 12 photos. She wants to put an equal number of photos on each of 3 pages. How many photos should she put on each page?

   _____

3. Carl took 48 photos on his camping trip. He wants to put an equal number of photos on 8 pages of his photo album. How many photos should he put on each page?

   _____

4. Eduardo has 63 photos of his friends. He wants to give an equal number of photos to 7 of his friends who are in the pictures. How many photos will each friend get?

   _____

5. Helena has a box of 78 family photos and a photo album with 10 pages. How many photos must she fit onto each page of the album to keep all of the family photos in one album?

   _____

   _____

6. Rae is buying film for her trip to Washington, D.C. Each roll of film costs $4. How many rolls of film can she buy with $25? Explain.

   _____ rolls.

   _____

   _____

   _____

Name _____ Date _____

Problem-Solving Practice

Algebra: Multiplication Properties and Division Rules

Solve.

1. Multiply. $3 \times 5 =$ _____

Then use the Commutative Property to write a different multiplication sentence.

_____

2. Multiply. $6 \times 8 =$ _____

Then use the Commutative Property to write a different multiplication sentence.

_____

3. There are 3 balls in a can of tennis balls. Write a multiplication sentence to show how many balls are in 4 cans.

_____

4. Karly has 2 model cars that are blue. She has 2 model cars that are red. She has 2 model cars that are silver. Write a multiplication sentence to show how many model cars she has.

_____

5. Inga has 3 packs with 2 pens in each pack. She has 2 packs with 3 pencils in each pack. Write two multiplication sentences to show how many pens and pencils she has.

_____

6. Ellie is using beads to make 7 bracelets. She puts 9 beads on 4 of the bracelets. She puts 8 beads on 3 of the bracelets. How many beads does she use?

_____

Name _____ Date _____

Problem-Solving Practice

Multiply and Divide Facts Through 5

Solve.

1. If you have 5 four-wheel trucks, how many total wheels are there?

   _____

2. If there are 4 books to a set and you have 5 sets, how many books do you have?

   _____

3. There were 4 schools that each had 7 classes attend a seminar. How may total classes were there?

   _____

4. There are 3 students on each relay team. How many teams would 15 students make?

   _____

5. If 2 boys each make 15 muffins for a bake sale, and there are 2 other people making 15 muffins each, how many total muffins will be for sale?

   _____

6. If you have a class of 24 children, how many groups of 4 can you make?

   _____

7. If you have a class of 35 students, how many groups of 5 can you make?

   _____

8. A teacher gave out 14 stickers a week for 4 weeks. How many stickers did she give away?

   _____

Name _____ Date _____

Problem-Solving Practice

Multiply and Divide Facts Through 10

Solve.

1. If you have 8 dogs, how many total legs are there? How many total eyes and ears?

   _____

2. If you have 4 pens to a set and you have 9 sets, how many pens do you have altogether?

   _____

3. There were 4 siblings that each visited the dentist twice a year. How many total times did they visit the dentist in 7 years? 8 years? 10 years?

   _____

4. There are 5 kids on each relay team. How many teams would 35 kids make?

   _____

5. If the boys make 7 toy cars to sell at a fund-raiser for $5 each, how much money will they raise?

   _____

6. If you have a belt that is 10 inches long, how long would 7 belts be?

   _____

7. If you have a basket of 9 strawberries, and you pick 5 more baskets with the same amount, how many berries are there altogether?

   _____

8. If you can fit 8 toy dinosaurs in a box, and you have 5 boxes, how many total toy dinosaurs do you have?

   _____

Name _____ Date _____

Problem-Solving Practice
Multiply with 11 and 12

Solve.

1. How many legs do 11 dogs have?

   _____

2. If you have 11 backpacks with 5 books in each one, how many total books are there?

   _____

3. There were 4 math tutors who each had 12 students to tutor in a day. How many students did they see altogether?

   _____

4. You have 8 sticks of gum to share among 10 friends. How many sticks of gum do you have to divide in half if you try to give each friend at least one piece of gum?

   _____

5. For every 12 cans you recycle, you receive 50¢. If your family collected 144 cans, how much money would you receive?

   _____

6. If you measure a room that is 11 feet × 12 feet, how many total square feet are there?

   _____

7. If you have a basket of 11 blueberries and you pick 8 *more baskets* with the same amount, how many berries are there altogether?

   _____

8. You can fit 12 model cars in a box. If you have 3 boxes, how many total cars do you have?

   _____

Name _____ Date _____

Problem-Solving Practice

Algebra: Multiply Three Numbers

Solve.

1. If you have a pet snake that he eats 2 times a week, how many

   times will you feed it in 6 weeks? _____

2. A teacher wanted to buy 4 new basketballs for each class in
   the school. There are 4 elementary classes and 5 middle-school
   classes in the school. How many basketballs would the teacher

   need to buy? _____

3. Jose rides 5 miles on his bike one way to school. How many miles

   will he ride in 10 days to and from school? _____

4. If 8 people fit in a row on an airplane, and there are 12 rows, how

   many people would fit into the plane? _____

5. A ferryboat can carry 24 people and allows 2 suitcases per person.
   How many suitcases can 4 ferryboats hold?

   _____

6. If you and 6 friends go on a roller coaster ride 5 times, and it is $2
   per person per ride, what is the total price you paid for rides?

   _____

7. How much would you spend if you went on a roller coaster 7 times

   with the same group of friends for the same price? _____

Name _____ Date _____

Problem-Solving Practice

Factors and Multiples

Solve.

1.  If you eat 2 eggs each day, how many eggs will you eat in 6 days? In 7, 8, and 9 days?

   _____, _____, _____, _____

2. A bird eats 7 berries a day. How many berries does it eat in 4 days? 5 days? 1 week?

   _____, _____, _____

3. A golf cart with two rows can carry 2 passengers in each row. If you have 6 carts, how many people can fit in them?

   _____

4. If you and a friend go to the park and pay $18 to rent bicycles,

   how much do you each owe? _____

5. Ramon is organizing the desks in his classroom. He wants them in equal rows and columns. How many ways can he organize the 15 desks in the classroom? List the factors.

   _____

   How many ways can he organize 32 desks? List the factors.

   _____

   How many ways can he organize 27 desks? List the factors.

   _____

6. A pet store has 4 dogs for sale. They have three times as many fish for sale, twice as many birds for sale, and half as many cats for

   sale. How many total animals are for sale? _____

5-1

Problem-Solving Practice

Addition and Subtraction Expressions

Solve.

1. Ming and Amy count the total number of beads they have. Ming has 21 beads. Write an expression to show the total number of beads that Ming and Amy have all together.

   _____

2. Julie has 16 paper clips. She gives away *x* number of paper clips. Write an expression for the number of paper clips she has left.

   _____

3. Each week, Hector sends 2 e-mails to his friend Chet. He also sends e-mails to other friends each week. Write an expression to show how many e-mails Hector sends each week.

   _____

4. George and his brother have a total of 8 CDs. If George has *n* CDs, write an expression to show how many CDs his brother has.

   _____

5. Delia saves $2 from her weekly allowance. She also saves the money she earns from delivering newspapers each week. Write an expression to show her total weekly savings. If she earns $5 delivering newspapers this week, how much money does she save in all this week?

   _____

5-2

Problem-Solving Practice

Solve Equations

Solve.

1. Tad had $10. He saved $2 more. Then he spent half of his money on a model car. How much money does he have left?

   _____

2. A large puzzle costs $6. A small puzzle costs $4. How much would you pay for 1 large puzzle and 2 small puzzles?

   _____

3. Nadine has 3 sets of CDs with 2 CDs in each set. She also has 15 other CDs. How many CDs does she have in all?

   _____

4. Emma has competed in 27 more swim meets than Peter. Peter has competed in 10 more swim meets than Spencer. If Emma has been in 42 swim meets, how many meets has Peter been in? How many meets has Spencer been in?

   _____

5. A store owner opens a case of 12 water bottles. He puts an equal number of bottles on each of 3 shelves in the display cooler. Then he puts 2 more bottles on each shelf. How many bottles of water are on each shelf?

   _____

6. Kameko gets on the school bus at 8:15 A.M. Every 3 minutes the bus makes a stop, and there are a total of 5 stops. Then the bus drives another 15 minutes to reach the school. What time does Kameko arrive at school?

   _____

7. On Saturday, Grant has 3 hours to work on his school projects. It takes him 5 minutes to record data for each of the 6 plants in his science project, and he spends 45 minutes on the chart he is making. How much time does he have left to work on his relief map for social studies?

   _____

Name _____ Date _____

Problem-Solving Practice

Identify, Describe, and Extend Patterns

Solve.

1. Abby runs every afternoon after school. On even numbered days she runs for 15 minutes. On odd numbered days she runs for 10 minutes. If Abby runs every day for 31 days, how many total minutes does she run? _____

2. Dustin and Michael are saving money to build a tree house. Dustin adds $5 to their piggy bank every other week. Michael adds $2 every week. So far they have saved $45. How many weeks have they been saving their money? _____

3. Allison practices the piano every day. What is the rule for the pattern shown in her practice log?

Piano Practice Log						
Day	1	2	3	4	5	6
Min	15	20	25	30	35	40

   _____

4. Every other month Kelly calls her grandmother. Kelly calls her cousin Tina in the months she doesn't speak to her grandmother. If Kelly calls her grandmother in January, will she call Tina or her grandmother in August? _____

5. Anna goes to the library every week in June and July. In the first and third weeks she checks out 7 books. In the second and fourth weeks she checks out 5 books. How many total books does she check out in June and July? _____

6. Janelle is making a beaded bracelet. She places a square bead first followed by 4 round beads. Will the 25th bead be a square or round bead? _____

Problem-Solving Practice

Function Tables: Find a Rule (+, −)

The table shows how many people will be going on a field trip.

Input (s)	Output (p)
25	29
27	31
29	
31	
33	

1. Jessica's class is going on a field trip. The school will bring all the students who are there that day plus 4 chaperones. Use the table to write an equation for this situation. _____

2. Find how many people will go if there are 29, 31, and 33 students going. _____

3. Write a new equation if the school will bring the students and 6 chaperones. _____

4. Create a table for the new equation. How many people will go if 35 students go on the trip?

Input (s)	Output (p)

_____

Name _____ Date _____

Problem-Solving Practice

Multiplication and Division Expressions

Solve.

1. Ming and Amy have 6 bags of beads. Each bag contains 14 beads. Define a variable and write an expression for the number of beads Ming and Amy have. Then solve the expression.

   _____

2. If Ming buys 3 more bags of beads, how many beads will Ming and Amy have altogether?

   _____

3. Julie's mother is 40 years old. She is 4 times as old as Julie. To find Julie's age, solve the equation $40 \div a = 4$, where a equals Julie's age.

   _____

4. Andrew has three boxes of holiday decorations. There are 25 decorations in each box. Write and solve an expression for the number of decorations in each box. Then solve the expression.

   _____

5. George and his brother have a total of 8 CDs. Each CD has the same amount of songs. If there are 120 total songs, how many songs are on each CD? Write an expression to find the number of songs on each CD. Then solve the expression.

   _____

6. Each student at Fairview Elementary keeps 3 books in his or her backpack. If there are 261 students at Fairview Elementary, how many total books are carried by the students? Write an expression to find the total number of books carried by the students. Then solve the expression.

   _____

Name _____ Date _____

Problem-Solving Practice

Function Tables: Find a Rule (×, ÷)

Jorge and his dad make sandwiches for a party. The table shows grilled cheese and turkey sandwiches.

Rule: _____	
Grilled Cheese Input (*c*)	Turkey Output (*t*)
4	1
12	3
20	5
28	
36	

1. Write an equation that describes the relationship between grilled cheese and turkey sandwiches.

_____

2. How many turkey sandwiches will Jorge make if he is making 28 grilled cheese sandwiches? _____

Chloe is helping plan the class field trip. Her teacher asked her to figure out how many students can come. The table shows the students and chaperones for the field trip.

Rule: _____	
Chaperones Input (*c*)	Students Output (*s*)
3	18
5	30
7	42
9	
11	

3. Write an equation that describes the relationship between chaperones and students. _____

4. How many students can come if 9 chaperones go on the field trip?

_____

5. How many people in all will go if 66 students go on the trip?

_____

30

Name _____ Date _____

Problem-Solving Practice

Multiples of 10, 100, and 1,000

Solve.

1. There were 20 pirates on a ship. Each one had 1 eye patch. How many eye patches were on the ship in all?

   _____

2. The pirates had 6 treasure chests with gold coins. Each chest had 9,000 gold coins. How many gold coins did the pirates have in all?

   _____

3. The pirates traveled 50 miles every day. They have been at sea for 8 days. How many miles have they traveled altogether?

   _____

4. One day the pirates sighted 2 whales every hour for 10 hours. How many total whales were sighted?

   _____

5. Over the 8 days that they have been at sea, the pirates ate 20 fish each day. How many fish were eaten in all?

   _____

6. The pirates plan to explore 3 islands which will require walking 20 miles per day. How many miles will they have walked if it takes 4 days to explore all 3 islands?

   _____

7. Four of the pirates have been away at sea for 200 days. How many days total have these four pirates been away at sea?

   _____

Name _Ellie_ Date _1/23/18_

Problem-Solving Practice

Use Rounding to Estimate Products

Estimate each product.

1. Each fourth-grade class has 25 students. There are three classes in the school. About how many fourth-grade students are there in all?

   90 fourth-graders.

2. Pens cost $1 each. Adam buys about 4 pens a week. About how much does he spend on pens in a month?

   _$20_

3. Chad wants to buy 6 different colored pencils. Each pencil costs 98¢. About how much will all of the pencils cost?

   _$6_

4. Habib drives about 79 miles a day for work. About much does he drive in a 5-day work weak?

   400 miles

5. A soccer player runs about 110 yards each game. After he has played 3 games, about how many yards has he run?

   300 yards

6. Erica has $5 to buy new folders. She wants 1 purple folder, 2 green folders, 1 red folder, and 5 blue folders. Each folder costs 49¢. Does she have enough money to buy all of the folders that she wants? Explain.

   Yes all of them total cost $4.50. There are 9 folders.

6-4

Problem-Solving Practice

Multiply Two-Digit Numbers

Solve.

1. There are 3 birds on the ground. Each bird eats 10 worms. How many worms are eaten all together?

   30 worms

2. Simon has 12 CDs. He burns 3 copies of each. How many CDs did Simon make?

   36 CDs

3. The school auditorium has 4 rows of seats. There are 18 seats in each row. How many students can sit in the auditorium?

   72 students

4. The school cafeteria has 6 rows of tables. Each row has 22 places to sit. How many students can eat in the school cafeteria?

   132 students

5. Scott is playing a game of memory with some picture cards. He makes 4 rows and puts 23 cards in each row. How many picture cards is Scott using in this game?

   92 cards

6. Kate would like to play the memory game, too. She adds her cards to the game. Now, there are 8 rows, and 24 cards in each row. How many cards are there now?

   192 cards

7. John wants to buy birthday gifts for 8 friends. He can spend $19 for each gift. How much will he spend in all?

   _$152_

8. Caroline makes $5 an hour pet-sitting for the neighbors. Last summer she worked 31 hours. How much money did Caroline earn?

   _$155_

Problem-Solving Practice

Multiply Multi-Digit Numbers

Solve.

1. The first floor of an apartment building has space for 112 small apartments. The next 5 floors are the same. The first 6 floors of the apartment building have space for how many apartments?

   _____

2. Each year 6,578 people eat lunch in a certain restaurant. During a period of 5 years, how many people will eat in this restaurant?

   _____

3. The maximum number of people that can be on the top of a building at one time is 400. By 8 A.M. one morning there were already 372 people on the top. The elevator was moving up with 37 more people. How many people will not be allowed off the

   elevator? _____

4. At a comedy club, amateur comedians get a chance to try out their jokes. A comedian can only try out once in a week, and each comedian has 15 minutes to try out. The comedy club is open 12 hours a day, 7 days a week. How many comedians can have a chance to try out in this club every week?

   _____

5. A famous concert hall seats 11,551 people. Every seat was filled for the 9 concerts that took place in June. How many people heard a concert in this concert hall in June?

   _____

6. A taxi driver kept track of how many people were friendly to him in a day. Sixteen people told him what they were doing in the city, 8 asked him if he had a family, 23 told him what they liked best about the city, and 3 asked if they could buy him coffee. The taxi driver wanted his friends to believe that people are friendly, so he tripled his numbers. How many people did the taxi driver say were friendly to him?

   _____

6–7

Problem-Solving Practice

Multiply Across Zeros

Solve.

1. Mr. Parker has 10 boxes of chalk. Each box has 12 pieces of chalk inside. How many pieces of chalk are there in all?

   _____

2. There are 401 windows in the school. Each window has 9 panes. When Mr. Parker washes each window pane by hand, how many panes does he wash?

   _____

3. The art teacher ordered 201 sets of markers for her students to use. Each set has 32 markers. How many markers did she order in all?

   _____

4. Each time the art class paints pictures, 108 brushes must be cleaned. If the art class paints pictures 9 times during the year, how many brushes will be cleaned?

   _____

5. Brent rode his bicycle 4 miles during the last day of August. His bicycle has an odometer that measures how far in miles and yards. Each mile has 1,760 yards. How many yards did Brent ride on the last day of August?

   _____

6. Cassandra ran 207 miles during the year. She wears a pedometer that measures how far she runs in miles and yards. Each mile has 1,760 yards. How many yards did Cassandra run in the year?

   _____

Name _____ Date _____

Problem-Solving Practice

Multiply by Tens

Solve.

1. Teams of 16 students are helping the town clean the park. There are 20 teams in all. How many students are cleaning the park?

   _____

2. Students are going on a field trip in 10 buses. Each bus carries 35 students. How many students can go on the field trip?

   _____

3. Mr. Parker arranged 1 car for every 5 students to travel to the zoo. A total of 40 cars were needed. How many students went on the trip?

   _____

4. It cost $8 to buy food for each class to feed the animals in the petting zoo. Mr. Parker bought food for 6 classes. How much did the food cost?

   _____

5. 1,056 animals live in the zoo. The 8 caretakers make sure that they each check on all of the animals each day. How many animals does each caretaker check each day?

   _____

6. 17 students run in a charity race to raise money for the zoo. Nine of the students each raise $20. The rest of the students each raise $30. How much did the students raise in all?

   _____

Name _____ Date _____

Problem-Solving Practice

Estimate Products

Solve.

1. Each of 32 classrooms has 4 computers. About how many computers are there in all?

   _____

2. A new keyboard for the computer costs $49. The school is buying 3 keyboards. About how much will they cost?

   _____

3. There are 42 times for students to work in the computer lab during one week. If 19 students can work in the computer lab at one time, about how many students can work in the computer lab during one week?

   _____

4. The school is buying 28 new computers for the computer lab. One computer costs $812. About how much will all of the computers cost?

   _____

5. The school district is buying laser printers for 62 schools. Each printer costs $1,198. About how much will all the printers cost?

   _____

6. The school district is buying software for virus protection. Each software package costs $48. There are 6,085 computers all together in the district's schools. About how much will the software cost?

   _____

Name _____ Date _____

Problem-Solving Practice

Multiply Two-Digit Numbers

Solve.

1. There are 15 students in each school club. There are 20 clubs in all. How many students are in all of the clubs? Multiply. Tell which method you used.

   _____

2. There are 15 students in the art club. By the end of the school year, each student had made 23 pictures. How many pictures did the students make in all? Multiply. Tell which method you used.

   _____

3. The fourth-grade students at Tremont School receive a ribbon if they read 50 books during the school year. There are 69 ribbons given out at the end of the year. How many books did the students read in all? Multiply. Tell which method you used.

   _____

4. There are 27 students in Mr. Jacob's class. By the end of the school year, each student will have completed 72 tasks on the class schedule. How many tasks will have been completed? Multiply. Tell which method you used.

   _____

5. The town's camera store bought 98 cameras for school photography clubs to use. Each camera cost $57. How much did the cameras cost in all? Multiply. Tell which method you used.

   _____

6. There are 35 students in the photography club at Columbus School. Each student was given enough rolls of film to take 46 photos. How many photos did the students take in all? Multiply. Tell which method you used.

   _____

Name _____ Date _____

Problem-Solving Practice

Multiply Three-Digit Numbers by Two-Digit Numbers

Solve.

1. Each art class uses 231 pipe cleaners for a project. How many pipe cleaners will 15 classes use? Multiply. Check that the answer is reasonable.

   _____

2. A box of art paper costs $15. How much do 220 boxes cost? Multiply. Check that the answer is reasonable.

   _____

3. Each week, 989 cars drive through the wildlife park. How many cars drive through the park in 24 weeks? Multiply. Check that the answer is reasonable.

   _____

4. A book about space exploration costs $18. There are 262 students in the school. How much will books for the whole school cost? Multiply. Check that the answer is reasonable.

   _____

5. The tile crew can lay 878 tiles in one day. How many tiles can the crew lay in 62 days? Multiply. Check that the answer is reasonable.

   _____

6. There are 981 floor tiles in one classroom in the school. How many floor tiles will it take to replace the tiles in 28 classrooms? Multiply. Check that the answer is reasonable.

   _____

Name _____ Date _____

Problem-Solving Practice

Multiply Greater Numbers

Solve.

1. Jamie visits her cousins twice a year. Each visit is 134 miles round trip. How many miles does Jamie travel to visit her cousins each

   year? _____

2. Three members of the crafts club are making necklaces. It takes 202 beads to make each necklace. How many beads will they

   need altogether? _____

3. Alexandra and her 3 friends decide to go to the movies. Each ticket costs $7. How much money will they need for the

   movies? _____

4. Jason is taking a bus to visit his grandparents. The bus trip is 113 miles each way. How many miles will Jason travel to and from his grandparents' house? Write the multiplication sentence and solve.

   _____

5. Jack is a pilot for a large airline. He plans on retiring in 8 years. Every week, he follows the same schedule of flights. He knows that he flies 78,434 miles each year. How many miles will he fly

   before he retires? _____

6. The city parks commission wants to build a new park. The model has 6 tennis courts. Each tennis court will cost $92,378. The city does not want to pay more than $550,000 for all 6 courts. How

   much will the tennis courts cost? _____

   Will the city be able to build all of them? _____

40

Name _____ Date _____

Problem-Solving Practice

Division with Remainders

Divide. Check each answer.

1. The zoo gives the nature club 47 wildlife posters. There are 20 members in the club. They want to divide the posters evenly among the members. How many posters will each member get? How many posters are left?

   _____

2. The science club has 43 members. Ms. Reed wants to divide them into groups of 10. How many groups of 10 will there be? How many groups will have an extra member?

   _____

3. 20 members of the ecology club are writing reports about trees. They have chosen 53 kinds of trees. Each member writes a report about the same number of trees. How many reports will each one write? How many members will have to write an extra report?

   _____

4. 10 members of the ecology club are also making leaf books. They will gather information about 44 kinds of leaves. How many leaves will each of the 10 members study? How many members will study an extra kind of leaf?

   _____

5. There are 63 endangered mammals in the U.S. Thirty students plan to research each mammal. If each student takes an equal number of mammals to research, how many mammals will they study? How many students will have an extra mammal to research?

   _____

6. 20 students want to learn more about endangered birds in the U.S. There are 76 endangered birds. If each of the students takes an equal number of endangered birds, how many birds will each student study? How many students will have an extra bird to study?

   _____

8-2

Problem-Solving Practice

Divide Multiples of 10, 100, and 1,000

Divide. Use patterns.

1. There are 30 people in Mr. Smith's class. Mr. Smith is taking his class to New York City. The total price of the trip is $30,000. How much will the trip cost each person? _____

2. The bus will travel 4,500 miles. 5 chaperones will take turns driving. If each chaperones drives the same amount, how many miles will each of the chaperones drive? _____

3. When the trip is over, Mr. Smith says that they will have spent a total of 80 hours driving in the bus, over a total of 10 days. How many hours will they average driving each day? _____

4. The plan is for the 30 students to be gone 20 days. 10 days will be spent sight seeing in New York City. Mr. Smith has set aside $6,000 for spending money while in New York City. How much money does each student have to spend each day while in New York City?

_____

5. For the 10 driving days, the 30 students will need a total of 150 motel rooms. How many students will stay in each room?

_____

6. For the 10 days in New York City, the 30 students will need a total of 75 hotel rooms. How many students will stay in each room?

_____

Name _____ Date _____

Problem-Solving Practice

Estimate Quotients

Estimate. Check your estimate.

1. 2,670 people attended rock concerts in a huge arena. There were 5 different bands playing with about the same number of people watching each band. About how many people attended each concert?

   _____

2. Jill earned 1,690 points in math class. Half of the points were for 8 tests. Jill scored about the same on each test. About how many points did she score on each test?

   _____

3. Besides the tests, the other 1,000 points in math class are homework and quizzes. The 20 quizzes and 20 homework assignments are all worth the same amount of points. About how much is each quiz worth?

   _____

4. Mr. Kirk graded 4,212 word problems. Each problem took about the same amount of time to grade. Mr. Kirk spent about 1,000 minutes grading the word problems. About how many problems did he grade per minute?

   _____

5. Mrs. Alex graded 639 tests during the school year. She had 30 students. About how many tests did each student take?

   _____

6. Mary is practicing for a math competition. She should be able to calculate about 18 problems within 180 minutes. About how long will she have for each problem?

   _____

Name _____ Date _____

Problem-Solving Practice

Two-Digit Quotients

Divide. Use estimation to check.

1. Pat earned $65. He worked 5 days. How much did he earn each

   day? _____

2. Pat's job was to feed and walk his neighbors' dog while they were
   on vacation. During the 5 days that he worked, he spent a total of
   150 minutes with the dog. How many minutes each day did he

   work? _____

3. Matt earned $60. He worked 4 days. How much did he earn each

   day? _____

4. Matt's job was to rake leaves. Each day it took him a total of
   3 hours to rake 2 yards. How long did he spend raking each yard?

   _____

5. Sam earned $70 helping his father paint the garage. He was paid
   per hour. If he spent 7 hours total helping his father, how much

   was he paid for each hour he worked? _____

6. Jason worked a total of 77 hours mowing lawns, pulling weeds,
   and raking leaves for the 7 houses on his street. How long did it
   take him to mow the lawn, pull the weeds, and rake each yard?

   _____

Name _____ Date _____

Problem-Solving Practice

Three-Digit Quotients

Divide. Use estimation to check.

1. Ann needs to read 415 pages in 5 days. How many pages should she read each day?

   _____

2. Jamal has read 567 pages in 9 hours. How many pages of the book did he read per hour?

   _____

3. Kendra was awarded $250 for her hard work. She gave several people $25 each for a total of $200. How many people did she give money to? How much money did she have left over?

   _____

4. Eric collected 140 children's books to give to a community center. The books were then divided equally between 7 families. How many books did each family receive?

   _____

5. For 6 months Ann and her friend Jamal spent 240 hours reading stories to first graders who came to the library. They spent the same amount of time reading each. How many hours did they spend reading each month?

   _____

6. Before Ann and John graduated from high school, they had read 1,520 stories to children. They read the same number of stories each time that they read to children. For 8 years they read to children. How many stories did they read each year?

   _____

8–8

Problem-Solving Practice

Quotients with Zeros

Divide. Use estimation to check.

1. The camping club spent $102 on 2 tents. How much did each tent cost?

   _____

2. The animal park sold 315 tickets in 3 days. If the same number of tickets were sold each day, how many tickets were sold?

   _____

3. Ms. Jones took 9 children to the water park. The children's tickets cost $108. How much did each ticket cost?

   _____

4. The water park had 1,320 visitors on Friday, Saturday, and Sunday. There were an equal number of visitors each day. How many visitors were there each day?

   _____

5. Ms. Lopez divided 103 students into 6 teams for relay races. How many students were on each team?

   _____

   _____

6. There are 2 large gym classes with 3 teams in each class. Each team needs an equal number of balls to play a game. There are 306 balls in all. How many balls will each team use?

   _____

8-9

Problem-Solving Practice

Divide Greater Numbers

Divide. Use estimation to check.

1. The hobby store had 3,126 beads. They put them into bags of 6 beads each. How many bags did they have?

_____bags

2. The hobby store had 4,212 beads. They put an equal number of beads into 8 boxes. How many beads were in each box?

_____ beads

How many beads were left over?

_____ beads left over

3. The community center is putting new floor tiles in 6 rooms. They have 2,250 floor tiles for all of the rooms. Each room is the same size. How many floor tiles will be used in each room?

_____ tiles

4. Best Floor Company has 8 orders for the same number of floor tiles. They have 8,965 tiles in stock to fill the orders. How many floor tiles are in each order?

_____ tiles

How many floor tiles will they have left?

_____ tiles left

5. The owner of the garden store ordered 9,636 packets of flower seeds. He stored the seeds by putting an equal number of packets into each of 6 bins. How many packets went into each bin?

_____

6. The garden store owner paid $6,472 for flower bulbs. She made 4 equal payments for the flower bulbs. How much did she pay each time?

$ _____

Name _____ Date _____

Problem-Solving Practice

Three-Dimensional Figures

Solve.

1. Molly has a set of wooden blocks. This is one of her blocks. Tell how many faces, edges, and vertices the block has.

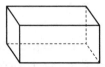

_____

2. Molly's set of wooden blocks also has a block that is a cylinder. How many bases does the cylinder block have? What geometric figure makes the bases?

_____

3. Natasha bought a large bead to hang from a necklace. The bead has 5 faces, 9 edges, and 6 vertices. What kind of figure was the bead?

_____

4. Mel has a board game that uses 10 pieces shaped like the one below. How many bases does each game piece have? Describe the shape of the bases.

_____

5. Iman and his father are making an end table for their living room. When they are done, the end table has 6 faces, 12 edges, 8 vertices. What kind of figure did Iman and his father make?

_____

_____

9–2

Problem-Solving Practice

Two-Dimensional Figures

1. Nick and his brother are building a tree house. It will have 2 windows. One window is shaped like a square, and the other is shaped like a rectangle. What do these two figures have in common?

_____

2. Nick's brother draws a 3-sided figure to show what the roof of the tree house will look like. Is it a polygon? If so, what kind of polygon?

_____

3. Sara is playing a chalk game on the sidewalk. She draws a large rectangle first. Inside the rectangle, she draws the same figure 10 times. The figure is not a polygon. What figure did she draw?

_____

4. Sara uses her chalk to draw a line diagonally through her rectangle. Now, instead of one quadrilateral, she has two of the same polygons. What figures did she make?

_____

5. For a homework assignment, Dina must find polygons around her town and draw them. She goes down to the harbor, where she sees a boat like the one below. She draws it, but the teacher says it is not a polygon. Why?

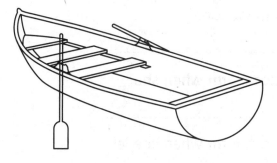

_____

_____

6. Sean used toothpicks to make the following figures: 2 triangles, 3 pentagons, 4 quadrilaterals, and 6 hexagons. How many toothpicks did he use?

_____

Name _____ Date _____

Problem-Solving Practice

Angles

Solve.

1. Matt looks at the clock and sees that it is 12:55. What type of angle do the hands of the clock form?

   _____

2. Now the hour is 1:00. Matt wants to wait until the hands of the clock form a right angle. Until what hour must he wait?

   _____

3. The clock in Ms. Alston's classroom reads 2:15. She tells the students that class will be over when the hands on the clock next form an obtuse angle, and the minute hand is pointing directly to a number on the clockface. What time will class be over?

   _____

4. Jake goes to a friend's house at 2:30. He stays until the hands on the clock form an acute angle. What is the earliest time he could have left?

   _____

5. Elise set her alarm clock for 50 minutes after 2 on the morning she was leaving for her camping trip. She fell back asleep for 10 minutes. She finally left the house at 3:25. What type of angle did the hands on the clock form when her alarm went off?

   _____

   What type of angle did the hands on the clock form when she

   woke up the second time? _____

   What type of angle did the hands on the clock form when she left

   the house? _____

6. Elise left her house at 3:25. She arrived at the trail head at 6:00. In the time it took Elise to arrive at the campsite, how many times did the hands on a clock form right angles?

   _____

Problem-Solving Practice

Triangles

Solve.

1. Jon's garden has 3 sides. None are equal sides and there are no equal angles. What type of shape is his garden?

   _____

2. Santi has 3 sticks and of them are 3 cm and one is 6 cm. Will he be able to make a triangle with them?

   _____

3. Brianne is making a design with geometric shapes. She draws a triangle that has 2 sides, 2 cm long. The triangle has 2 angles that are 70°. On a separate sheet of paper, draw a triangle like the one Brianne has drawn. What kind of triangle is it—isosceles, equilateral, or scalene?

   _____

   _____

4. If you draw an equilateral triangle and two sides are 3 inches, what is the length of the third?

   _____

5. Bruno is making a drawing of the Pentagon. How many triangles will he need to draw to make this polygon, and how many sides will it have?

   _____

6. Alison is cutting out fabric. One side of the material is 10 ft, another side is 6 ft, and the third side 8 ft. What shape is she cutting?

   _____

Name _____ Date _____

Problem-Solving Practice

Quadrilaterals

Solve.

1. Bonnie draws a quadrilateral with 4 equal sides, and 4 right angles. What quadrilateral is it?

   _____

2. Santi's wallet is in the shape of a rectangle. Two sides are 2 inches long. The other 2 sides are 3 inches long. Chaz's wallet has the same measurements but is not a rectangle. What other shape could it be?

   _____

3. Marcus draws a quadrilateral that has 4 equal sides, but no right angles. What quadrilateral might it be?

   _____

4. Andy draws a square. Peter draws another shape that has 4 equal sides. Peter says his shape is square. Andy says it is not. What other shape might Peter have drawn?

   _____

5. Cassidy places two right triangles together to form a quadrilateral. What type of quadrilateral might she have formed?

   _____

6. Alison is cutting out fabric. The top of the material measures 1 ft, and the bottom measures 3 ft. Each side measures 2 ft. What shape is she cutting?

   _____

Name _____ Date _____

Problem-Solving Practice

Locate Points on a Number Line

Solve.

1. A number line starts with 989 and ends with 1,003. It is marked with intervals of 1. The letter *T* is halfway between 989 and 1,003. What is the value of *T*?

_____

2. Rita's mother was born in 1960. In 1990, she married Rita's father. In 1995, she gave birth to Rita. Create a number line of these events. Use intervals of 5 years on your number line.

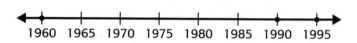

1960 1965 1970 1975 1980 1985 1990 1995

3. A timeline shows that Amelia Earhart was born in 1897. The timeline shows that in 1928 Amelia flew for her first time over the ocean. How old was Amelia when she took this flight?

_____

4. A number line starts with 191,005 and ends with 191,025. It is marked with intervals of 5. The letter *N* is halfway between 191,005 and 191,025. What is the value of *N*?

_____

5. A number line starts with 110,000 and ends with 210,000. It is marked with intervals of 10,000. The letter *W* is halfway between 110,000 and 210,000. What is the value of *W*?

_____

6. Create a number line that starts on an odd number and has a scale of 3.

_____

Name _____ Date _____

Problem-Solving Practice

Lines, Line Segments, and Rays

Solve.

1. Jenna is waiting for her piano teacher to come at 6:30. She looks at the clock and sees that it is 6:00. Do the hands on the clock form a line, line segment, parallel lines, or intersecting lines?

   _____

2. Jenna looks at the clock at 3:00. Do the hands on the clock form a line segment, parallel line segments, or perpendicular line segments?

   _____

3. Ryan's ski instructor tells him that he should keep his skis parallel. Draw how Ryan's skis should look.

4. Ryan accidentally crosses the tips of his skis and falls down. What word describes the type of line that Ryan's crossed skis created?

   _____

5. Louis gets lost on the way to Josh's house. He calls and says he is on Main Street. To get to Josh's house from Main Street, Louis must turn left on First Avenue. Is First Avenue parallel to Main Street?

   _____

6. Josh lives at the corner of First Avenue and Maple Street. How might he describe the way the streets meet at his house?

   _____

   _____

   _____

Name _____ Date _____

Problem-Solving Practice

Find Points on a Grid

Use the grids to solve.

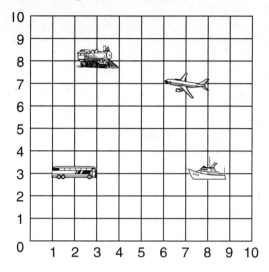

1. Lindsay made a grid of the transportation centers in her town. Give an ordered pair to tell the location of the boat dock.

   _____

2. Use the grid. Name the place located at (2, 3).

   _____

3. Five students made a grid for a group project. They mapped the location of each of their homes and their school. Use the grid. Give an ordered pair for the location of Carlos' house. Give an ordered pair for where Kimi lives.

   _____

4. Use the grid to name the location for each of these ordered pairs:
   (2, 2); (6, 4); (1, 8)

   _____.

Make a grid on a separate sheet of paper to solve.

5. Graph these ordered pairs on graph paper: (3, 2); (4, 4); (5, 2); (5, 7); (6, 4); (7, 2). What do you notice about the numbers you graphed?

   _____

   _____

   _____

   _____

Name _____ Date _____

Problem-Solving Practice

Rotations, Reflections, and Translations

1. Jean saw the sign below. Is the second *E* a translation, reflection, or rotation of the first *E*?

   _____

2. Carrie and Levis are playing checkers. Carrie says the checkerboard squares are transformation. What kind of transformation are the squares on the checkerboard? Explain.

   _____

   _____

   _____

   _____

3. While Sam was in the car on his way to his aunt's house, he saw a sign that said, "DO NOT PASS." Sam read the sign and then noticed that something was different about the second S is the word PASS. It was backwords. Would the second S be a translation, reflection, or rotation of the first S.

   _____

4. Allison draws a picture of a flower. She draws a circle for the center of the petals. Keeping her pencil on the circle, she draws the petals out around it. What type of transformation are the petals?

   _____

5. Mirabel and her family are camping at the lake. Mirabel and her sister walk to the jetty on the lake. The last sign reads "JETTY," but Mirabel notices the second *T* is upside down. Is the second *T* a translation, reflection, or rotation of the first *T*?

   _____

6. David is cutting a heart shape out of construction paper. First he folds the paper in half. Then he cuts out the heart shape and unfolds it. What kind of transformation did David make?

   _____

10–7

Problem-Solving Practice

Congruent Figures

Tell whether the figures appear to be congruent. Write *yes* or *no*.

1. Amy drew these two figures on dot paper. Look at the figures. Are they congruent?

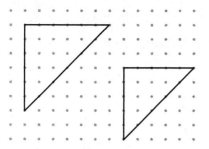

_____

2. Hamid looked at the ends of two wooden blocks. Are they congruent?

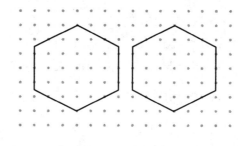

_____

Copy each figure on dot paper. Then draw one congruent figure.

3. Next, Amy drew the right triangle below. On a separate sheet of dot paper, copy the figure. Then, draw one congruent figure.

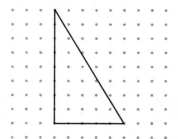

4. Hamid traced the end of another wooden block onto dot paper. The figure he traced looks like this. On a separate sheet of dot paper, copy the figure. Then, draw one congruent figure.

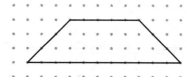

5. Inez wants to make two pentagons. On a separate sheet of dot paper, draw two congruent pentagons.

_____

10-8

Problem-Solving Practice

Symmetry

Solve.

1. The pattern on Beth's floor is in the shape of a plus sign. She copies the shape onto paper and draws a dotted line through the center. Is the dotted line a line of symmetry?

   _____

2. Sam is painting a picture of his mother. If he wants to make sure her face is symmetrical in the painting, what can he do to the

   canvas before he begins? _____

   _____

   _____

3. Sheila draws this flower with 6 petals. Then she draws a dotted line through the center of her flower as shown here to find out whether the flower is symmetrical. Is the dotted line a line of symmetry on Sheila's flower?

   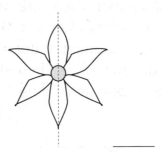

4. How many lines of symmetry can you draw through a square? _____

5. Mirabel is drawing a picture of a flower she found near their campsite. The flower has 5 petals. She draws a dotted line through her flower. Is the dotted line Mirabel drew a line of symmetry? How can you tell without drawing it?

   _____

   _____

   _____

   _____

Problem-Solving Practice

Customary Units of Length

Solve.

1. Kelly has six notebooks, each $1\frac{1}{2}$ inches thick. If she stacks the notebooks together, how tall would the stack be?

   _____

2. Clark says that his parents' car is 96 units long. Jay says that his parents' car is 8 units long. Which customary unit of length was each person using?

   _____

3. Thomas says that a tree in his yard is a mile high. Is his claim reasonable? Explain.

   _____

   _____

4. What customary unit of length would you use to measure the following item? Then measure the item to the nearest half unit.

   _____

5. Tony's car gets 25 miles per gallon of gasoline. He needs to drive 100 miles, and he has 3 gallons of gasoline. Does he have enough gasoline? If not, how many miles can he travel on 3 gallons of gasoline?

   _____

6. List two tools used to measure length and provide a situation in which that tool would be useful.

   _____

   _____

11-2

Problem-Solving Practice

Convert Customary Units of Length

Solve.

1. Rosa is 64 inches tall. Kathleen is 5 feet 4 inches tall. Who is taller?

   _____

2. The school is 27 yards away from the public library. Additionally, the school is 108 feet away from the train station. Which is the school closer to, the library or the train station?

   _____

3. Amani is standing 15 feet from the water fountain. Dimitri is standing 132 inches from the water fountain. Who is standing closer to the fountain?

   _____

4. Alex says he walks 30,000 feet to school every morning. Is his claim reasonable? How many miles is 30,000 feet?

   _____

5. Morgan says that her brother is 2 yards tall. How many feet tall is he? How many inches?

   _____

6. Write a real-world problem involving the conversion of customary lengths. Give your problem to a classmate to solve.

   _____

Name _____ **Date** _____

Problem-Solving Practice

Metric Units of Length

Solve.

1. Carlos says that the distance from Chicago to Dallas is about 3,000 kilometers. Is he correct? Explain how you know.

   _____

   _____

2. During a walk on the beach, James and Mira see a crab. Mira estimates that the crab is 20 meters long. Is her estimate correct? Explain.

   _____

   _____

   _____

3. Sonia is standing 20 centimeters from the door. Dominic is standing 20 meters from the door. Who is standing farthest from the door?

   _____

4. Benjamin sees a horse on his aunt's farm that is 2 meters long. Name three other things that are about 2 meters long.

   _____

5. Sheri says she walks 300 millimeters to school every morning. Is her claim reasonable? Explain.

   _____

   _____

   _____

6. Explain why it would be better to measure the length of a stapler in centimeters instead of meters.

   _____

   _____

   _____

11–5

Problem-Solving Practice

Measure Perimeter

Find the perimeter of each figure.

1. Jorge is drawing a design for an airplane. He draws this triangle to use as a wing on the airplane. Find the perimeter of the wing.

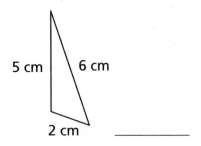

5 cm   6 cm

2 cm   _____

2. The Hitoshi family plans to make a short sidewalk and patio in their backyard. First, they will need to place a frame around the space. This drawing shows the shape and dimensions of the frame they need to place. What is the frame's perimeter?

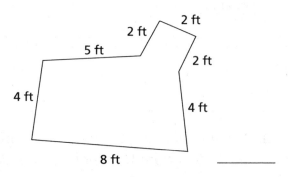

2 ft   2 ft

5 ft

2 ft

4 ft

4 ft

8 ft   _____

3. Jorge uses this rectangle as a pattern for a picture of a building. What is the perimeter of his rectangle?

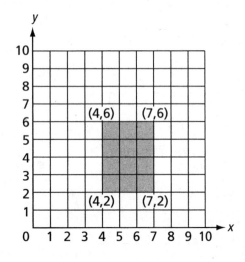

4. Mrs. Hitoshi decides to plant a flower bed next to the patio. She wants to use an iron border around the flower bed. She uses this grid to find out how many sections of iron border she will need. Find the perimeter of the flower bed.

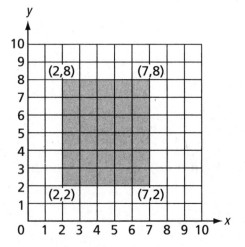

_____   _____

Name _____ Date _____

Problem-Solving Practice

Measure Area

Find the area of each figure.

1. Lin and her sister are getting a new rug for their bedroom. The rug is 3 feet wide and 5 feet long. Find the area of the rug. _____

2. Lin wants to use blue tissue paper to decorate the top of a box that is 4 inches square. What is the area of the piece of tissue paper Lin needs?

   _____

3. Ms. Charles wants to carpet the reading nook shown here. How many square meters of carpet will Ms. Charles need for the reading nook? _____

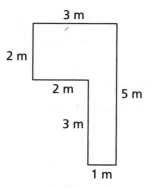

4. Helena makes a canvas for an oil painting. Use graph paper to draw the shape of her canvas with length 12 centimeters and width 6 centimeters. Tell what shape Helena's canvas is, and find the area.

   _____

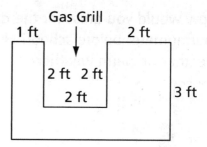

5. Mike needs to know what size can of water sealer to buy to cover his deck. There is a built-in gas grill on the deck, so he will seal only the area around the grill shown here. Find the area of the deck that Mike will use water sealer on. _____

6. Mike's sister wants to make a cover for the gas grill on the deck. She has a piece of waterproof fabric that is 4 feet long and 1 foot wide. Use graph paper to draw a figure with length 4 feet and width 1 feet. Tell what the figure is, and find the area. Then tell what shape the section of the deck with the gas grill is and find the area. Will the piece of waterproof fabric cover the grill?

   _____

   _____

   _____

   _____

   _____

11-8

Problem-Solving Practice

Measure Temperature

Solve.

1. How would you dress for the day if you looked at the following thermometer before school? Hint: would you dress for cold weather or warm weather?

_____

2. Michelle and Isaac each read a thermometer outside on a cool spring day. Michelle says it is 40°F outside. Isaac says it is 100°F outside. Who is correct? Explain your reasoning.

_____

_____

3. Is it more reasonable to say that a glass of cold water would be 40°F or 150°F? Explain.

_____

_____

_____

4. Does the line on the thermometer go up or down when the temperature gets hotter? What about when the temperature gets colder?

_____

_____

_____

5. The average June temperature in Mario's hometown is 75°F. Is this a cool temperature or a warm temperature?

_____

6. Name two situations in which you might see a thermometer being used.

_____

_____

Name _____ Date _____

Problem-Solving Practice

Customary Units of Capacity

Choose the most reasonable estimate.

1. Katie is pouring herself a drink of juice. Is it reasonable to say that Katie will pour about 8 fluid ounces of juice? Explain.

   _____

   _____

2. Zach is filling his dog's bowl with water. Is it reasonable to say that Zach will need about 4 gallons of water? Explain.

   _____

   _____

3. LeTara is filling her swimming pool with water. Is it reasonable to say that LeTara will need about 100 cups of water? Explain.

   _____

   _____

4. Wes is pouring himself some ketchup to go with his potato wedges. Is it reasonable to say that Wes will need 2 fluid ounces? Explain.

   _____

   _____

5. If there are 8 fluid ounces in 1 cup, how many fluid ounces are there in 2 cups?

   _____ fluid ounces

6. Name two things in the grocery store that are about one quart.

   _____

   _____

12-2

Problem-Solving Practice

Converting Customary Units of Capacity

Solve.

1. Myndi can buy a 2-pint container of strawberries for $4.75 or a 1-quart container for $4.25. Which is the better buy? Explain.

   _____

   _____

   _____

2. Dina can buy a 270-fluid ounce can of paint for $10 or a 2-gallon can of paint for $10. Which is the better buy? Explain.

   _____

   _____

3. Chris can buy a 16-fluid ounce bottle of shampoo for $2.79 or a 2-cup bottle of shampoo for $2.99. Which is the better buy? Explain.

   _____

   _____

   _____

4. Ashley can buy 3 pints of orange juice for $2.25 or 5 cups of orange juice for $2.25. Which is the better buy? Explain.

   _____

   _____

5. Ella can buy 2 quarts of milk for $3 or 1 gallon of milk for $3. Which is the better buy? Explain.

   _____

   _____

6. Jorge can buy a 16-fluid ounce bottle of water for $1.50 or a 2-cup bottle of water for $1. Which is the better buy? Explain.

   _____

   _____

   _____

Name _____ Date _____

Problem-Solving Practice

Metric Units of Capacity

1. Emily has an ear infection. She puts 4 milliliters of ear drops in each ear. Is that reasonable? Explain.

_____

_____

2. Ryan fills his cat's water bowl with 2 milliliters of water. Is that reasonable? Explain.

_____

_____

3. Eva is helping her mother cook pasta. Her mother pours 2 liters of water into a pot. Is that reasonable? Explain.

_____

_____

4. Amara brings an energy drink with her to soccer practice. It is in a 1-milliliter bottle. Is that reasonable? Explain.

_____

_____

5. How many liters are in 9,000 milliliters? Explain how you found your answer.

_____

_____

6. Identify 4 objects in the grocery store that can hold less than 10 milliliters.

_____

_____

12–4

Problem-Solving Practice

Customary Units of Weight

Solve.

1. Jesse claimed that his goldfish weighs about 2 pounds. Is Jesse's claim reasonable? Explain why or why not.

   _____

   _____

2. Tasha claimed that her skateboard weighs about 3 pounds. Is Tasha's claim reasonable? Explain.

   _____

   _____

3. Charlie claimed that a baseball weighs about 5 ounces. Is Charlie's claim reasonable? Explain why or why not.

   _____

   _____

   _____

4. Is it reasonable to say that 10 baseballs weigh more than a ton? Explain why or why not.

   _____

   _____

5. Which animal's weight is closer to 1 pound: a lion or a robin?

   _____

6. List three objects in the grocery store than weigh about 1 pound.

   _____

   _____

Problem-Solving Practice

Converting Customary Units of Weights

Solve.

1. The world's largest carrot weighed 18 pounds 13 ounces. How many ounces did this carrot weigh?

   _____ oz

2. The world's largest squash was 962 pounds. How many more pounds would the squash need to weigh in order to weigh 1 ton?

   _____ lb

3. The world's largest pumpkin pie weighed 2,020 pounds. About how many tons would 5 of these pies weigh?

   _____ T

4. Refer to Exercise 3. How many ounces did the world's largest pumpkin pie weigh?

   _____ oz

5. The world's largest pumpkin was 1,385 pounds. The world's heaviest cabbage was 1,984 ounces. Which vegetable was bigger? Explain.

   _____

   _____

6. The world's largest apple weighed 59 ounces. Did this apple weigh more than 4 pounds? Explain.

   _____

   _____

Name _____ Date _____

Problem-Solving Practice

Metric Units of Mass

Solve.

1. The table lists the masses of fruits and vegetables. Complete the chart by writing a reasonable mass for each object.

Mass of Fruits and Vegetables	
Object	Mass (g or kg)
grape	1 ☐ ____
pumpkin	2 ☐ ____
apple	150 ☐ ____
large potato	1 ☐ ____

2. A banana's mass is about 130 grams. Rita is buying 5 bananas at the grocery store. What will be the total mass of Rita's bananas?

_____

3. Cantaloupe costs $1 per kilogram. If Rob is buying a cantaloupe, is it reasonable to say that he will spend $10? Explain.

_____

_____

_____

4. Julio is buying a carton of blueberries that has a mass of 100 grams. Is it reasonable to say that there are 150 blueberries in Julio's carton? Explain.

_____

_____

_____

_____

5. Wade has change in his pocket. It has a mass of 10 grams. What coins could Wade have in his pocket?

_____

_____

6. Name four living things that have a mass of less than 1 kilogram.

_____

_____

Name _____ Date _____

Problem-Solving Practice

Estimate and Measure Volume

Solve.

1. Mrs. Wong and Mr. DeVore each have a box of tissues on their desks. Mrs. Wong's box is 4 units long, 2 units wide, and 3 units tall. Mr. DeVore's box is 5 units long, 1 unit wide, and 3 units tall. Whose box has a greater volume?

   _____

2. Brady and Sheree are both building block towers. Brady's tower is 4 units long, 3 units wide, and 7 units tall. Sheree's tower is 5 units long, 2 units wide, and 6 units tall. Whose box has a greater volume?

   _____

3. A swimming pool has a length of 20 units, a width of 7 units, and a depth of 10 units. What is the volume of the swimming pool?

   _____

4. A refrigerator has a length of 3 feet, a width of 2 feet, and a height of 6 feet. What is the volume of the refrigerator?

   _____

5. Give the dimensions of a rectangular prism that has a volume of 70 cubic units.

   _____

6. Give two possible sets of dimensions of a rectangular prism that has a volume of 36 cubic units.

   _____

   _____

Name _____ Date _____

Problem-Solving Practice

Elapsed Time

The table shows the zoo's daily schedule of activities.

Daily Activity Schedule	
Activity	Time
Lion Feeding	9:00 A.M.
Monkey Show	10:30 A.M. and 2:45 P.M.
Dolphin Show	11:05 A.M. and 3:25 P.M.
Bird Feeding	4:50 P.M.
Bat Show	7:00 P.M. and 8:00 P.M.

Solve.

1. Rachel attended the second monkey show. If the show ended at

   3:30 P.M., how long did it last? _____

2. Ozzy attended the bird feeding. It lasted for 25 minutes. What time

   did it end? _____

3. Neel wants to attend the first monkey show, which lasts
   45 minutes. Will he also be able to attend the first dolphin show?
   Explain.

   _____

   _____

4. The bat show is 35 minutes long. If Jai arrived at the zoo at
   1:15 P.M. and stayed until the end of the second bat show, how

   much time did he spend at the zoo? _____

5. How long is your school day? Draw clocks to support your answer.

   _____

6. Create a word problem that uses elapsed time.

   _____

Name _____ Date _____

Problem-Solving Practice

Parts of a Whole

Solve.

1. Tony lost a button off his shirt. He measures one of the remaining buttons to find out what size button to buy to replace the one he lost.

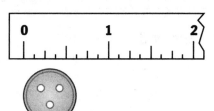

   Find the width of Tony's button and write a fraction for the part of an inch.

   _____

2. Diallo baked a pumpkin pie. He sliced it into 6 pieces. His family ate 5 of the pieces. Write a fraction to show what part of the pie the family ate.

   _____ of a pie

   Write a fraction to show how much of the pie is left.

   _____ of a pie

3. Alani has a pizza that is cut into 8 slices. After she and her friends finish eating, there are 3 slices left. Write a fraction that names the part of the pizza that is left.

   _____ of a pizza

4. Ciro has finished 1 part of his homework assignment. There are 3 parts to the assignment. What fraction of his assignment has he completed?

   _____

   Use grid paper to draw a rectangle and shade it to show how much of the assignment Ciro has finished.

5. Megan has read 4 chapters of a book about electricity. There are 8 chapters in the book. Use grid paper to draw a rectangle and shade it to show how much of the book Megan has read. If she reads two more chapters, what fraction of the book will she have read?

   _____ of the book

6. Jesse has a block of cheddar cheese. He cuts it into 12 equal chunks and puts toothpicks into them to serve at a party. After the party, Jesse discovers that 11 cheese chunks have been eaten. Write a fraction to show what part of the block of cheese that was eaten.

   _____ of the cheese

Name _____ Date _____

Problem-Solving Practice

Parts of a Set

Solve.

1. Lara saw 3 snowmen on her way to school. She noticed that 2 of the three snowmen were smiling. On a separate sheet of paper, draw a picture of the snowmen that Lara saw. Then write a fraction that describes the number of snowmen who are smiling.

   _____

2. Ali has a group of 9 game pieces. Some of them are white and some of them are not.

   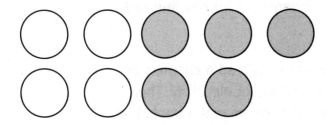

   Write a fraction that shows the part of Ali's game pieces that are

   white. ____

3. Diane has laid out 12 game cards. She put 7 of the cards face up and 5 of the cards face down. Write a fraction that names the part

   of Diane's cards that are face up. ____

4. James spends 2 hours a day doing homework. What fraction of

   the day does James spend on homework? ____

5. There are 8 students in the chess club. Only 7 of the members attended the last meeting. Write a fraction that tells what part of

   the chess club missed the meeting. ____

6. There are 32 bottles of milk on the grocery store shelf. Carrie buys 5 of the bottles and Heather buys 11 of them. What fraction of the original number of milk bottles is left after Carrie and Heather

   make their purchases? ____

13-4

Problem-Solving Practice

Equivalent Fractions

Solve.

1. Ms. Andrews has an umbrella that is gray and white. Look at the top of her umbrella.

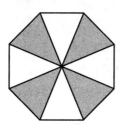

What fractional part of the umbrella is gray?

_____

Write an equivalent fraction.

_____

_____

_____

2. Dean has 10 marbles. He gives 2 of them to Jamie. Write a fraction for the number of marbles Dean has left.

_____

3. Lainie delivers newspapers. She spends $\frac{4}{12}$ of her earnings on a new CD. Write an equivalent fraction to show the amount of Lainie's earnings that she spends.

_____

_____

4. There are 32 students in Mr. Simon's class. Four of the students are on the soccer team. Write the fraction that shows how many of Mr. Simon's students are on the team.

_____

5. Ms. Ashton's class set 9 major goals for their school year. They have reached 6 of their goals. Write a fraction that names the goals that have been reached.

_____

Then write 2 equivalent fractions.

_____

_____

6. There are 72 players in the soccer league and 54 of the players are new this year. Write a fraction that shows the number of players who are new this year.

_____

Name _____ Date _____

Problem-Solving Practice

Compare and Order Fractions

Solve.

1. Lon can have $\frac{2}{3}$ cup of orange juice or $\frac{3}{4}$ cup of milk. Which amount is more?

   _____

2. Patti has three glue sticks that are partially used. One has $\frac{1}{5}$ left, one has $\frac{3}{5}$ left, and one has $\frac{3}{10}$ left. Order the fractions from *least* to *greatest*.

   _____

3. Eduardo has three cans of paint. One can is $\frac{3}{8}$ full, one is $\frac{3}{4}$ full, and one is $\frac{2}{16}$ full. Order the cans from *greatest* to *least* amounts of paint.

   _____

4. Samuel is making bread and needs $\frac{5}{8}$ cup of flour. Jason is making a different kind of bread and needs $\frac{3}{4}$ cup of flour. Who needs the greater amount of flour?

   _____

5. Lola measures three buttons to find one which will fit the buttonhole on the shirt she is making. One is $\frac{3}{16}$ inch, one is $\frac{3}{8}$ inch, and one is $\frac{1}{4}$ inch. Order the button sizes from *largest* to *smallest*.

   _____

6. Jerilyn has finished $\frac{27}{32}$ of her math problems. Matt has finished $\frac{7}{8}$ of his math problems. Who has finished the greatest number of math problems?

   _____

13-6

Problem-Solving Practice

Mixed Numbers

Solve.

1. Ana has 13 crayons that are only $\frac{1}{3}$ as long as they used to be. Rename $\frac{13}{3}$ as a mixed number.

   _____

2. Vic needs $1\frac{1}{2}$ cups of flour to bake bread. How many halves is that?

   _____

3. Pedro uses $\frac{1}{9}$ of a sheet of art paper to make one paper crane. He makes 75 cranes. How many sheets of art paper does Pedro use to make the cranes? Rename $\frac{75}{9}$ as a mixed number.

   _____

4. Jenny needs $3\frac{2}{3}$ cups of flour to bake bread. How many thirds is that?

   _____

5. The hardware company uses $\frac{1}{81}$ of a roll of wire to make a hook. The company made 351 hooks on Tuesday. How many rolls of wire did they use? Write your answer as a mixed number.

   _____

6. Tamika uses $\frac{1}{4}$ of a block of wax to make a candle. How many blocks of wax does she use to make 22 candles? Write your answer as a mixed number.

   _____

Name _____ Date _____

Problem-Solving Practice

Tenths and Hundredths

Solve.

1. Three-tenths of the students who use the recreation center play in the softball league. What is this fraction as a decimal?

   _____

2. About half of the students who play soccer also play basketball. What is this number as a fraction? As a decimal?

   _____

3. It has been a dry summer in Texas. Last Thursday, nine-hundredths of an inch of rain finally fell in the town of Conway. What is this as a decimal?

   _____

4. Tony spent $\frac{3}{4}$ as much time practicing on his piano as he spent practicing soccer. How much time is that in decimal form?

   _____

5. Last winter, it snowed two and a half inches in the town of Pratt. When the snow melted, the weather station recorded the total precipitation as twenty-three hundredths of an inch. How could they have expressed this as a decimal?

   _____

6. Liam called 5 parks one Sunday. He discovered that 3 of them were being used for soccer matches. What would that be as a fraction?

   _____

   As a decimal?

   _____

   Suppose Liam had called 100 parks. If he discovered $\frac{3}{5}$ of them were being used for soccer matches, how many parks would that be?

   _____ parks

14–2

Problem-Solving Practice

Relate Mixed Numbers and Decimals

Solve.

1. The school bell rings for 7 and $\frac{21}{100}$ of a second. What is the decimal form for how long the bell rings?

   _____

2. Jana used graph paper to show how many miles it is from her house to school. If each grid is equal to one mile, how far is Jana's house from school?

   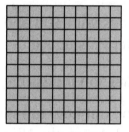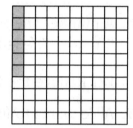

   Write the answer as a mixed number and a decimal.

   _____miles

3. In a speed-skating race, the winning skater's time was $\frac{435}{100}$ seconds faster than the second-place skater. What is the decimal for this fraction?

   _____

4. Alan used graph paper to show the length of the ring on his cell phone. If each grid is equal to one second, what is the length of the ring? Write the answer as a mixed number in simplest form and a decimal.

   _____

   _____

5. Judy and Trish read that the total rainfall in their town was, "two and thirty-four hundredths of an inch." Judy wrote that fraction as $2\frac{34}{100}$ inches. Trish wrote it as $2\frac{17}{50}$ inches. Who was right? Explain.

   _____

   _____

   _____

   _____

   Using decimal form, how much rainfall did their town receive?

   _____

Name _____ Date _____

Problem-Solving Practice

Locate Fractions and Decimals on a Number Line

Solve.

1. Richard is making a table. He measures a piece of wood to make a table leg. On his ruler, there are 7 marks between each inch. The piece of wood ends at the 6th mark between 21 and 22 inches. How long is the piece of wood? Reduce the fraction if possible.

   _____

2. A number line starts with 500 and ends with 501. In between are 9 marks. The letter *W* is above the 7th mark. What is the value of

   W? Reduce the fraction if possible. _____

3. Alice wants to find out how tall she is. Her mother has her stand against a wall and she marks Alice's height. The ruler Alice's mother uses has 15 marks between each inch. Alice's height is at the 4th mark between 53 and 54 inches. How many inches tall is

   Alice? Reduce the fraction if possible. _____

4. A number line starts with 13 and ends with 14. In between are 31 marks. The letter *N* is above the 4th mark. What is the value of

   N? Reduce the fraction if possible. _____

5. A number line starts with 7 and ends with 9. In between are 7 marks. The letter *A* is above the 5th mark. What is the value of

   A? Reduce the fraction if possible. _____

6. Explain how to plot 7.5 on a number line.

   _____

   _____

   _____

   _____

14–5

Problem-Solving Practice

Compare and Order Decimals

Solve

1. Enrique averages 6.8 assists per game. Lorena averages 7.2 assists per game. Gilberto averages 5.9 assists per game. Who averages the most assists?

   _____

2. Many kids grow an average of 1.4 inches a year. If you grew 2.8 inches and your friend grew 1.2 inches, who grew more? Who was closer to the average amount?

   _____

3. If California received 2.1 inches of rain in January, 2.4 inches of rain in February, and 1.8 inches of rain in March, how much total rain did they receive? List the months in order of the most to least rain.

   _____

4. Martina played tennis for 3.5 hours on Saturday. She played for 2.5 hours on Sunday. Which day did she play the longest?

   _____

5. Olivia scored an average of 15.8 points a game, James scored an average of 17.1 points, and Joaquin scored an average of 18.4 points per game. Who had the best average? _____

6. Sean played a game of cards in an average of 14.3 minutes. After practicing his average changed to 13.8 minutes. Did his average improve? _____

7. Lauren, Kim, and Jackie each had different heights in centimeters. Compare their heights and list them from the shortest to tallest.

Name	Height (cm)
Lauren	167.64
Kim	152.4
Jackie	161.54

   _____

Problem-Solving Practice

Fraction and Decimal Equivalents

Name _____ **Date** _____

Solve

1. Katarina made biscuits. She needed to use $2\frac{1}{4}$ cups of flour for 12 biscuits. If she made 24 biscuits, how much flour did she use written as a decimal?

   _____

2. Louis made a snack with bananas and crackers for his 2 friends and himself. He used 2 bananas and 9 crackers. How much banana did each person get if it was divided evenly? Write your answer as a fraction.

   _____

3. If California received an average of 14.1 inches of rain in 2006, Arizona received an average of 10.8 inches of rain, and Nevada received an average of 9.9 inches of rain, which was the state that received the most rain? Write the amount as a fraction.

   _____

4. Thomas collects trains. He has 7 blue trains and $\frac{23}{30}$ are other colors. How many trains does Thomas have altogether?

   _____

5. Miriam has 100 buttons in her sewing basket. 28 of them are red, 52 of them are white, 10 are blue, and 10 are black. Write a fraction and a decimal to show how many red and white buttons she has.

   _____

6. There are 52 cards in a deck. $\frac{1}{4}$ of them are hearts, $\frac{1}{4}$ are spades, $\frac{1}{4}$ are diamonds, and $\frac{1}{4}$ are clubs. Write a fraction and decimal to show all the red cards.

   _____

14–8

Problem-Solving Practice

Decimals, Fractions, and Mixed Numbers

Solve.

1. Ana has 13 crayons that are only $\frac{1}{3}$ as long as they used to be. Rename $\frac{13}{3}$ as a mixed number in simplest form.

_____

2. Vic needs $1\frac{1}{2}$ cups of flour to bake bread. How many halves is that?

_____

3. Ramon surveyed 100 students about what sport they liked best. Seventy-five of the students liked soccer best. How can Ramon write that in a fraction?

_____

   How can he write it as a decimal?

_____

4. In his survey, Ramon found that $\frac{20}{100}$ of the students liked basketball best. How can Ramon write this in simplest form? How can he write it as a decimal?

_____

5. The hardware company uses $\frac{1}{81}$ of a roll of wire to make a hook. The company makes 351 hooks on Tuesday. How many rolls of wire do they use? Write your answer as a mixed number in simplest form.

   _____ rolls of wire

6. Tamika uses $\frac{1}{4}$ of a block of wax to make a candle. How many blocks of wax does she use to make 22 candles? Write your answer as a mixed number in simplest form.

   _____ blocks of wax

15–1

Problem-Solving Practice

Round Decimals

Solve.

1. Jennifer spent 6.34 hours at the beach today. How long did she spend at the beach, rounded to the nearest whole hour?

   _____

2. In the 1968 Olympics, Mike Burton from the U.S. swam the 400-meter freestyle race in 4.09 seconds. What is his speed rounded to the nearest tenth?

   _____

3. Amy and Kate decide to count the sidewalk squares between their houses. They count exactly 43.34. To the nearest tenth, how many squares are between their houses?

   _____

4. The record for the discus throw at Westlake High School is 30.58 meters. What is this distance rounded to the nearest whole number?

   _____

5. Jon is making a bookshelf unit the exact length of one wall. His measurements show that the wall is 67.027 inches long. If Jon rounds this number to the nearest hundredth and cuts pieces of wood that long, how long will each piece of wood be?

   _____

   Will the shelf fit in the room if he does this?

   _____

6. In the 2000 Olympics, Marion Jones from the U.S. ran the 200-meter race in 21.84 seconds. At her track meet, Sara runs it in 32.76 seconds. Round each speed to the nearest tenth.

   _____ seconds, _____ seconds

   About how much faster was Marion Jones than Sara?

   about _____ seconds

Name _____ Date _____

Problem-Solving Practice

Estimate Decimal Sums and Differences

Solve

1. The train trip from New York, NY to Washington, D.C. takes 3.4 hours. The trip from New York to Norfolk, VA takes 7.6 hours. About how much longer does it take to get to Norfolk?

   _____

2. Mr. Jones needs a bag of fertilizer and a bag of pine chips for his garden. A bag of fertilizer costs $8.98 and a bag of pine chips costs $5.13 at the garden store. About how much will Mr. Jones pay?

   _____

3. Ellie wants to practice skating in a straight line. She chalks a line on the sidewalk that is 15.75 meters long. Then she adds another 14.25 meters to her line. About how long is Ellie's line now?

   _____

4. Nadya has picked up $15.25 worth of art supplies at the hobby store. She puts back a sketch pad that costs $4.98. About how much money will the items cost now?

   _____

5. Jeannie wants to buy a jacket that costs $26.83. Her mother agrees to pay $15.70 of the total amount. About how much money does Jeannie need to buy the jacket?

   _____

6. Roger spent $43.07 on materials to build a small skate ramp. He spent $76.83 on materials to build a large skate ramp. About how much did Roger spend on the skate ramps altogether?

   _____

Name _____ Date _____

Problem-Solving Practice

Add Decimals

Solve.

1. Talia walked 0.36 miles to the store. Then she walked 2.3 more miles to her grandmother's house. How many miles did she walk in all? Check for reasonableness. _____

2. A small puzzle costs $2.06. A large puzzle costs $3.21. How much would you pay for both puzzles? _____

3. Iris wants to buy a model airplane kit that costs $6.29. She also wants to buy a model car kit that costs $3.89. How much will she pay for both model kits? Check for reasonableness.

   _____

4. A ribbon company produces 31.467 meters of silk ribbon per hour and 2.198 meters of velvet ribbon per hour. In all, how many meters of ribbon do they produce in an hour?

   _____

5. The Winters family is going to a museum. It costs $0.90 for a round-trip bus ticket. It costs $8.75 for a monthly bus pass. Mr. Winters buys a monthly bus pass into the city for himself and his wife because they use them to go to work. He buys his two children round-trip tickets for that day. How much did he pay for his bus tickets? Check for reasonableness.

   _____

6. On Monday, Ms. Tipton braided 7.325 yards of material for a handmade rug during her regular work hours. She braided another 0.907 yard when she worked an hour of overtime. How much material did she braid on Monday?

   _____

15–6

Problem-Solving Practice

Subtract Decimals

Solve.

1. Petra has $1.78 in her pocket. She spends $0.25 on a banana. How much money does she have left?

   _____

2. Abu weighs his book bag. It weighs 11.65 pounds. He takes out the dictionary and weighs it. The dictionary weighs 3.31 pounds. If he leaves the dictionary out, how much will the book bag weigh?

   _____

3. Celia has $16.41 saved. She wants to buy a book that costs $8.56. If she buys the book, how much money will she have left?

   _____

4. Andrea buys a roll of ribbon that is 13.859 meters long. She needs 2.9 meters of ribbon to decorate a picture frame. How much ribbon will she have left?

   _____

5. The computer game that Parker wants to buy costs $21.07 with tax. He has $17.86. How much more money does he need to buy the game?

   _____

6. Clarissa uses 12.064 meters of string to weave a big bag. She uses 9.142 meters of string to weave a smaller bag. How much more string does she use for the big bag?

   _____